BEARS

LEARN & PLAY

EVERY DAY!

This book belongs to

Published by Wishing Well Books,
an imprint of Joshua Morris Publishing, Inc.,
355 Riverside Avenue, Westport, CT 06880.
Copyright © 1992 Oyster Books.
All rights reserved. Printed in Hong Kong.
ISBN: 0-88705-775-6
2 4 6 8 10 9 7 5 3

WISHING WELL BOOKS & DESIGN is a registered trademark
of The Reader's Digest Association, Inc.

Grateful thanks are due to Lizzy Pearl for her assistance
during the very early stages of this book's development.
Rhymes © Jenny Wood and Ali Brooks 1992.

BEARS
LEARN & PLAY
EVERY DAY!

Written by Jenny Wood
Illustrations by Rebecca Archer

WISHING WELL BOOKS®

Say hello to the Bears.
Can you say all their names?

The Bears are learning that some things go together.
Here are some that you might know.

soap and washcloth

toothbrush and toothpaste

undershirt and underpants

hat and coat

Try to say the words out loud.

paint and paintbrush

bowl and spoon

bat and ball

pail and shovel

Can you think of any other things that go together?

The Bears do different things at different times of the day.
Early in the morning, the Bears eat breakfast.

What do you like to eat for breakfast?

After breakfast, the Bears play with their toys.

What is Tiny Bear doing?
Which of your toys do you like best?

Before the Bears go to bed, they have a bath.
They love the warm water.

Do you like having a bath?

After their bath, it is time for
the Bears to go to bed.
Gray Bear reads a bedtime story.
But White Bear has fallen asleep.
What is your favorite bedtime story?

The Bears are learning that each part of the body has its own name.
Do you know the names of the parts of the body White Bear is pointing to?

eyes

nose

ears

mouth

Try to say the names out loud.

Here is Big Bear. Where are his eyes?
Where is Big Bear's nose?
Where are Big Bear's ears?
Where is Big Bear's mouth?

Can you point to your own eyes, nose, ears, and mouth?

Say the names of these parts of the body out loud, too.

arms

Can you wave your arms in the air, just like the bears?

hands

Hold up your hands. What do you use your hands for?

legs

Point to your legs. What do you do with your legs?

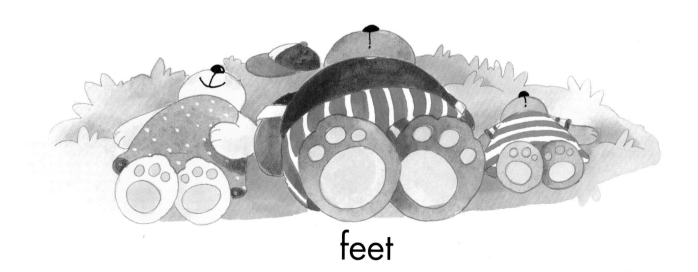

feet

Each bear has two feet. How many feet do you have?

tummy

Where is your tummy? Can you find your belly button?

bottom

Where is your bottom? Can you bounce on your bottom?

Here is a rhyme about parts of the body.
Say the rhyme out loud and do what the words say.
Do you know the names of any other parts of the body?

Hands clap,
Legs jump,
Arms wave,
Feet thump.

Ears listen,
Eyes twinkle,
Mouths smile,
Noses wrinkle.

Heads nod,
Tummies wriggle.
Can you make
Your bottom wiggle?

The Bears are moving in different ways.
Big Bear is walking on tiptoe.
Brown Bear is bouncing on a chair.
Tiny Bear is crawling along the floor.

Can you move like the Bears?

Yellow Bear and Black Bear
are climbing on a chair.
Some of the Bears
are rolling on the rug.

The Bears are going home for a snack.
Yellow Bear and Small Bear are walking.
Black Bear and Panda Bear are running.

Can you hop like Brown Bear?
Which bear is jumping?
And who is skipping?

The Bears are having fun making different sounds.

laughing

Big Bear is laughing.
Do you laugh
when you are tickled?

White Bear is whispering.
Can you whisper, too?

whispering

Black Bear is kissing Yellow Bear.
Can you make the sound of a kiss?

kissing

singing

These bears are singing.
Do you like singing?
What song do you like best?

White Bear and Panda Bear
are clapping.
Can you clap your hands?

clapping

These bears are stamping.
Can you stamp your feet?

stamping

splashing

These bears are splashing in the water.
Do you like splashing?

banging

Bang, bang, bang goes Big Bear on his drum.
Yellow Bear and Panda Bear are joining in.
Can you make a banging sound?
What other sounds can you make?

Tiny Bear's birthday

Tiny Bear is excited.
Today is her birthday.

The Bears have given her
lots of presents.

Tiny Bear wants to play hide and seek in the backyard.
She wants to hide first.

Can you see where Tiny Bear is hiding?
The Bears cannot find her.

Gray Bear is angry.

Big Bear is worried.

Small Bear is sad.

But Tiny Bear is safe.
Panda Bear finds her hiding behind the flowers.
Did you spot where Tiny Bear was hiding?

The Bears are happy.
They are all together again.

"Come on," says Big Bear.
"It's time for a snack. I'm hungry."
The other Bears are hungry, too.

Big Bear has made a special birthday cake.
Tiny Bear has two slices.
Do you like eating birthday cake?

The Bears are tired.
It has been an exciting day.

And Tiny Bear is
very, very sleepy.

Bears can tiptoe,
Bears can creep.
Bears can run and jump and leap.

Bears can whisper,
Bears can talk.
Bears can whistle while they walk.

Good-bye!

See you in the next book.

Bears are happy,
Bears are glad.
Bears are good and never bad.